ALTERNATOR
BOOKS™

UNEXPLAINED

BLOODTHIRSTY VAMPIRES

Craig Boutland

Lerner Publications ◆ Minneapolis

Lerner Publications Company
A division of Lerner Publishing Group, Inc.
241 First Avenue North
Minneapolis, MN 55401 USA

For reading levels and more information, look up this title at www.lernerbooks.com.

Main body text set in Minion Pro.
Font provided by Adobe Systems.

Library of Congress Cataloging-in-Publication Data

Names: Boutland, Craig, author.
Title: Bloodthirsty vampires / Craig Boutland.
Description: Minneapolis : Lerner Publications, 2019. | Series: Unexplained
    (Alternator Books) | Includes bibliographical references and index.
Identifiers: LCCN 2018050615 (print) | LCCN 2019006468
    (ebook) | ISBN 9781541562929 (eb pdf) | ISBN 9781541562868 (lb : alk. paper) |
    ISBN 9781541573826 (pb : alk. paper)
Subjects: LCSH: Vampires—Juvenile literature.
Classification: LCC BF1556 (ebook) | LCC BF1556 .B68 2019 (print) | DDC 398/.45—
    dc23

LC record available at https://lccn.loc.gov/2018050615

Manufactured in the United States of America
1-46413-47502-4/2/2019

Contents

Introduction

Stories about vampires have been around for thousands of years. Vampires are undead creatures that come out of their graves at night. They drink the blood of living things, especially humans. At dawn, vampires return to their graves. Daylight destroys their powers and makes them weak.

Real or Imaginary?

While there are stories about vampires living in lonely castles in the mountains, there is no real evidence that vampires exist. For some, vampires are just a **myth**. Other people believe they need to protect themselves from vampires. They say that certain things, like holding garlic or a Bible, can scare vampires away.

Vampires in History

Belief in vampires may have come from a simple misunderstanding. When people die, their bodies often appear bloated. This is because gas is trapped inside the stomach. Sometimes there are also traces of a red liquid around the person's mouth. In ancient times, when people saw dead bodies, they may have thought they were bloated from drinking blood.

The bones of about six million bodies lie beneath the city of Paris in France. Many were victims of the Black Death.

There are many stories of vampires from the Middle Ages (about 500-1500). Some stories were connected to the Black Death. This was a deadly **plague** that spread across Europe from 1347 to 1352. The plague killed between 30 and 60 percent of Europe's population. People believed that the disease was spread by the dead leaving their graves at night and infecting living people by biting them.

The bloodthirsty goddess Kali from Hindu mythology could be interpreted as a vampire. Her necklace is made from human skulls.

Worldwide

There are stories about bloodsucking **demons** from all over the world. In Hebrew mythology, Lilu was said to suck the blood from babies. In the Philippines, there is a story about a vampire who appears as a girl by day. However, at night she grows a long tongue and sucks the blood from sleeping victims. In West Africa, there are tales of a vampire-like creature with iron teeth and hooks for feet.

Many people in North America believed in vampires during the 1800s. In 1892, people in Rhode Island dug up the grave of nineteen-year-old Mercy Brown. She had recently died. People thought she was a vampire who was making her brother, Edwin, sick. They burned her heart and tried to make a **potion** from the ashes to heal her brother. In fact, both Mercy and Edwin had died from **tuberculosis**.

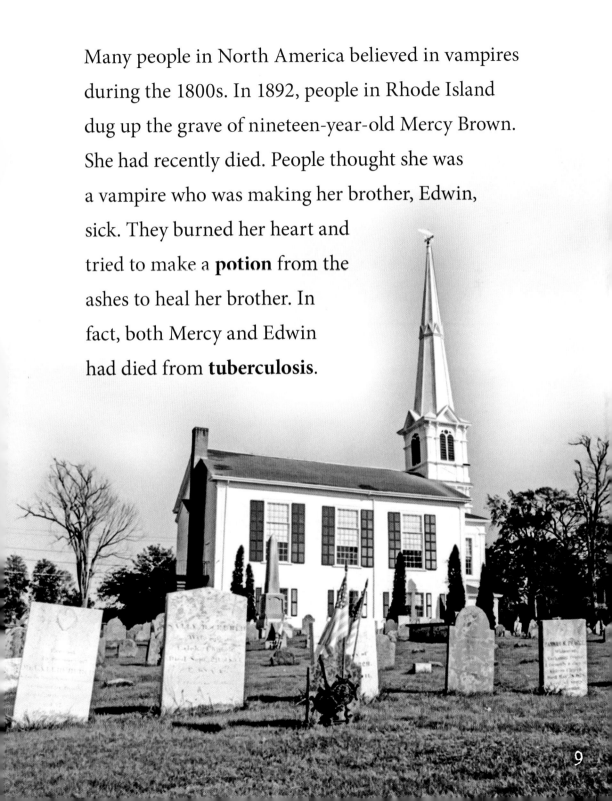

Vampires in Southeastern Europe

In 2013 a girl in a Romanian village started dreaming that her dead uncle was attacking her. The villagers dug up the uncle's body and found what looked like blood around his mouth. They thought this was proof that he was vampire. They cut off his head and buried the headless body at a crossroads. In the **folklore** of many countries, crossroads are places where people can seek protection from vampires.

Vampire stories come from all over the world.
The countries of southeastern Europe—Romania,
Bulgaria, Serbia, Albania, and Hungary—have
the most ancient stories. These countries had rulers
who inspired many vampire stories. They killed
thousands of innocent people in their cruel,
bloodthirsty hunger for power.

Protection From Vampires

Vampires do not have shadows or reflections.
In the Middle Ages, European villagers used garlic
and wild roses to protect themselves from vampires.
In Christian villages, holy items such as Bibles
or crosses were used.

Killing a vampire usually involved driving a wooden stake through its heart. But some people wanted to help the undead move on to the spirit world. In Germany, graves were dug up. The head of the vampire was cut off and placed between its feet. People believed this allowed the soul to leave Earth.

Vlad the Impaler and Countess Bathory

Vlad Dracul, or Vlad the Dragon, was the ruler of Wallachia, now modern-day Romania. His son, Prince Vlad III, was called Dracula, which means son of Dracul. When Vlad III captured enemies, he impaled them on stakes outside his castle. He became known as Vlad the Impaler. There are also stories that he drank the blood of his enemies.

Vlad the Impaler was imprisoned in Bran Castle in Transylvania in 1462. He had been captured by an enemy army.

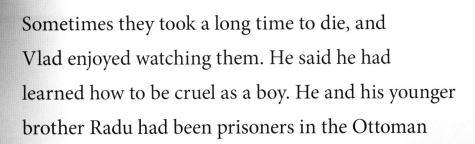

Sometimes they took a long time to die, and Vlad enjoyed watching them. He said he had learned how to be cruel as a boy. He and his younger brother Radu had been prisoners in the Ottoman Empire, an empire that existed in southeastern Europe and modern-day Turkey between 1300 and 1922. Vlad was a real person, but his cruelty and name, Dracula, became part of the folklore of Romania and Transylvania.

Was the beautiful Countess Elizabeth Bathory a bloodthirsty vampire? Or was she just an evil human being?

Vampire Countess?

One hundred years after Vlad the Impaler, there were stories of another bloodthirsty ruler in southeastern Europe. Countess Elizabeth Bathory of Transylvania was a well-educated woman. She married her husband in 1575 and had four children. They seemed like a normal **aristocratic** couple.

When Countess Bathory's husband died in 1604, she turned into a monster. The countess claimed that drinking the blood of young girls kept her looking young. She began killing her female servants. Later, she invited young women to her castle and killed them. No one knows exactly how many people she killed, but it was probably over one hundred. Some reports say it was over five hundred.

The ruins of Cachtice Castle, where Countess Bathory killed her **victims**. It is also where she was imprisoned and died in 1614.

Elizabeth Bathory drank the blood of her young victims. Some of her servants helped her. They were later put on trial.

Eyewitnesses

Was Elizabeth Bathory a vampire? Witnesses claimed they saw her drinking blood. There were other witnesses who said she even bathed in blood. In a country where vampire stories were common, there were many people who said she was a vampire.

Useful Bloodsuckers

Some bloodsucking animals have been used by doctors. Leeches are wormlike creatures that suck human blood. Leeches have been used in medicine for 2,500 years. In ancient times, doctors believed that if a leech sucked out a patient's blood, it would cure the patient. Today leeches are still used for some types of surgery.

Small Bats, Big Appetites

Vampire bats are small bats that live in Mexico as well as Central and South America. They have needle-sharp teeth that can pierce the thick skin of cattle and horses. Heat-seeking noses point the bats toward blood flowing beneath the skin. Vampire bats do not kill, but they carry **rabies**.

Animal or Vampire?

In 1995, several sheep were found dead on the island of Puerto Rico. They all had three holes in their chests. These holes were much bigger than **punctures** made by vampire bats. A woman said she saw the animal that attacked the sheep. She said it had spines on its back and did not have any hair. It hopped like a kangaroo.

The first reported sighting of a bloodsucking creature in Puerto Rico was near El Yunque National Forest.

No one found what had attacked the sheep on Puerto Rico. Over the next ten years, other attacks were reported in Latin America and Texas. People in Mexico called the mysterious vampire animal *el chupacabra*, which means "the goatsucker." Eventually, farmers found some dead animals that seemed to clear up the mystery.

They found dogs, raccoons, and coyotes that had all suffered from mange. This is a disease caused by bloodsucking **mites**. Mange makes animals scratch and pull out their fur. It makes them look very strange. It also makes them weak and sick. If a dog with mange killed a sheep, it would not have the strength to eat the meat. The dog could probably only manage to drink some blood before moving on.

This **mummified** chupacabra is on display in Calico, California.

Vampires Today

In 1819, an English writer named John Polidori wrote a short story called *The Vampyre*. This was the first modern vampire story published in English. Polidori had been the doctor of the poet Lord Byron. The vampire in Polidori's story, Lord Ruthven, was based on Byron. Since then, there have been thousands of books about vampires. Hundreds of films and TV programs about vampires have also been made.

Actor Christopher Lee played the bloodthirsty Count Dracula in ten films, including *Taste the Blood of Dracula* (1970).

Bram Stoker's Dracula

The most well-known vampire book
was written by Bram Stoker in
1897. He called the book *Dracula*.
The story was based on the legend
of Vlad the Impaler. The book
tells the story of Dracula's
journey from Transylvania
to England. In England,
Dracula finds new blood.
Stoker's book established many
ideas about vampires. In Stoker's
book, vampires live for centuries and
lose their powers in daylight.
Dracula returns to his coffin
after drinking blood.

Caught on Film

The first vampire films were made in the 1920s.
Some of the most famous were made in the 1960s
and 1970s. They represented vampires in a particular
way. The vampire usually wore a suit and a cape.
Dracula looked like an ordinary man until he
opened his mouth to reveal his fangs. Vampire
representations in the twenty-first century are very
different. On TV, one of the most successful vampire
series was *Buffy the Vampire Slayer.* Vampires are
now often grouped together with other bloodthirsty
beings such as zombies or werewolves.

Do You Believe in Vampires?

There are many ways in which people try to protect themselves from vampires. Whether vampires exist or not, the thought that a vampire might drink our blood while we sleep is scary.

We do not know if vampires exist. But we do know that some people believe in them.

Glossary

aristocratic: part of the highest-ranking group of people in a region

bloated: swollen with fluid or gas

catacombs: underground burial chambers

demons: evil spirits

folklore: the customs, beliefs, stories, and sayings associated with a particular group of people or a place

impaled: pierced through

mites: small arachnids that often carry disease

mummified: the dried, preserved body of a person or animal

myth: a traditional story for which there is no scientific proof or explanation

potion: a liquid with healing, magical, or poisonous properties

punctures: small holes made by pointed objects or teeth

rabies: a rare but serious disease infecting the brain and nervous system. It is mainly spread through a bite from an infected animal, such as a dog, foxes, raccoon, or bat.

undead: a dead body that has come back to life

Further Information

Bran Castle: Count Dracula, the Myth
http://www.bran-castle.com/dracula.html

Kidzworld: The Legend of Vampires
https://www.kidzworld.com/article/24861-the-legend-of-vampires

Mason, Jennifer. *Vampire Myths*. New York: Gareth Stevens Publishing, 2018.

Seigel, Rachel. *Vampires*. Mendota Heights, MN: Focus Readers, 2018.

Shea, Therese. *Bloodsucking Vampire Bats*. New York: Gareth Stevens Publishing, 2016.

Culture Trip: Vampires Around the World
https://theculturetrip.com/north-america/usa/articles/how-do-vampires-differ-around-the-world/

Index

Photo Acknowledgments

The images inside this book are used with permission of: ©Shutterstock/donates, p. 1; ©istockphoto.com /inhauscreative, p. 4-5; ©Shutterstock/Creatureart Images, p. 4-5; ©Shutterstock/Daniel Samek, p. 6-7; ©istockphoto.com/Danilerab, p. 8; ©istockphoto.com /J.C. Marcinak, p. 9; ©Shutterstock/volcano, p. 10; ©Shutterstock/Chad McDermott, p. 11; ©Shutterstock/ASHSTUDIO, p. 12; ©Shutterstock/Odette Villarrealn, p. 13; ©Shutterstock/ Valentin Balen, p. 14-15; ©Shutterstock/photoserbia, p. 15; ©Topfoto/World History Archive, p. 16; ©Shutterstock/ TTstudios, p. 17; ©iStockphoto.com /LightFieldStudiosa, p. 18; ©iStockphoto.com/Joel Carillet, p. 19; ©iStockphoto.com/szefel, p. 20-21; ©Shutterstock/ belizar, p. 22; ©Thinkstockphotos.com, p. 23; ©Public Domain, p. 24; ©Shutterstock/Paolo Rvo, p. 25; ©Alamy/TCD/Prod.DB, p. 26-27; ©Shutterstock/leolintang, p. 28; ©Shutterstock/ Nadezhda Manakhova, p. 29.

Front Cover: ©iStockphoto.com/serpeblu

Brown Bear Books has made every attempt to contact the copyright holder.
If anyone has any information please contact licensing@brownbear.co.uk